SUPER SIMPLE BODY

INSIDE THE STOMACH

KARIN HALVORSON, M.D.

Consulting Editor, Diane Craig, M.A./Reading Specialist

A Division of ABDO
ABDO
Publishing Company

VISIT US AT WWW.ABDOPUBLISHING.COM

Published by ABDO Publishing Company, a division of ABDO, P.O.
Box 398166, Minneapolis, Minnesota 55439. Copyright © 2013 by
Abdo Consulting Group, Inc. International copyrights reserved in all
countries. No part of this book may be reproduced in any form without
written permission from the publisher. Super SandCastle™ is a
trademark and logo of ABDO Publishing Company.

Printed in the United States of America, North Mankato, Minnesota
102012
012013

 PRINTED ON RECYCLED PAPER

Editor: Liz Salzmann
Content Developer: Nancy Tuminelly
Cover and Interior Design: Anders Hanson, Mighty Media
Photo Credits: Shutterstock, Thinkstock

Library of Congress Cataloging-in-Publication Data
Halvorson, Karin, 1979-
 Inside the stomach / Karin Halvorson ; consulting editor, Diane Craig,
reading specialist.
     p. cm. -- (Super simple body)
Audience: 4-10.
 ISBN 978-1-61783-614-5
1. Stomach--Juvenile literature. 2. Digestion--Juvenile literature. I.
Title.
 QP151.H38 2013
 612.3'2--dc23
                                 2012030858

Super SandCastle™ books are created by a team of professional
educators, reading specialists, and content developers around five
essential components—phonemic awareness, phonics, vocabulary,
text comprehension, and fluency—to assist young readers as they
develop reading skills and strategies and increase their general
knowledge. All books are written, reviewed, and leveled for guided
reading, early reading intervention, and Accelerated Reader®
programs for use in shared, guided, and independent reading
and writing activities to support a balanced approach to literacy
instruction.

NOTE TO ADULTS

THIS BOOK is all about encouraging children to learn the science of how their bodies work! Be there to help make science fun and interesting for young readers. Many activities are included in this book to help children further explore what they've learned. Some require adult assistance and/or permission. Make sure children have appropriate places where they can do the activities safely.

Children may also have questions about what they've learned. Offer help and guidance when they have questions. Most of all encourage them to keep exploring and learning new things!

CONTENTS

YOUR BODY

YOUR STOMACH

You're amazing! So is your body!
Your body has a lot of different parts. Your
eyes, ears, brain, stomach, lungs, and heart
all work together every day. They keep you
moving. Even when you don't realize it.

Do you wonder what happens to food after you eat it?

Your body breaks food into small pieces. Then it takes **nutrients** from the food. The nutrients go into your blood.

Your body doesn't need all of the food. It gets rid of the extra. This happens when you poop!

Food takes a long trip through your body. Your stomach is just one stop. This process is called digestion (DYE-JES-CHUHN).

CAN YOU THINK OF OTHER WAYS THAT YOU USE YOUR STOMACH?

ALL ABOUT DIGESTION

Your body needs energy. You get energy from food. Your body turns food into energy.

{ FAST FACT }

YOU'LL EAT ABOUT 50 TONS OF FOOD DURING YOUR LIFETIME.

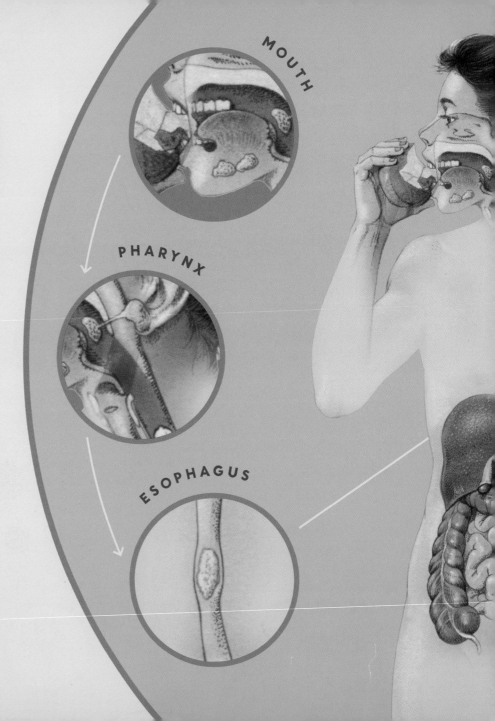

MOUTH

PHARYNX

ESOPHAGUS

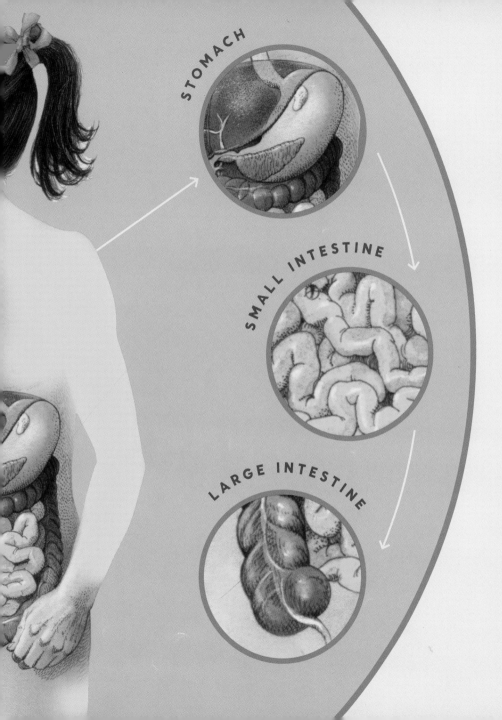

STOMACH

SMALL INTESTINE

LARGE INTESTINE

Your body has many
parts that help digest
food. They make up
your digestive (DYE-
JES-TIV) system.

Your digestive system
starts with chewing. It
ends with pooping. A lot
happens in between.

7

CHOW DOWN

Digestion starts with eating. Food has **nutrients**. The nutrients give you energy!

Fats, proteins, and sugars are types of nutrients.

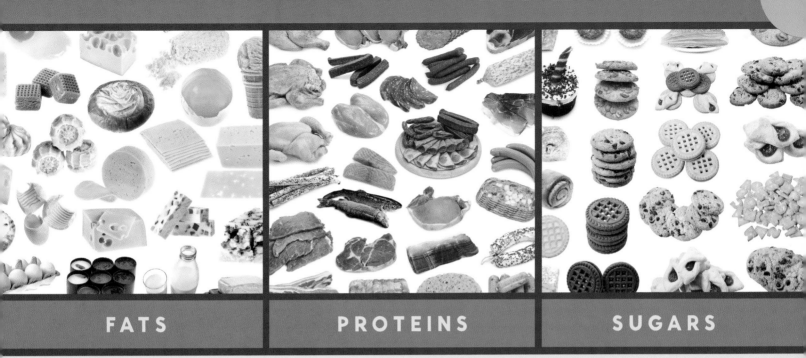

FATS

PROTEINS

SUGARS

Fats have a lot of energy. That's usually a good thing. But you shouldn't eat too much! Your body stores extra fat for later. Cheese, oil, butter, and nuts have a lot of fat.

Proteins are the building blocks of your body. They can also be used for energy. Meats, **beans**, and seeds are high in protein.

Sugars give your body energy quickly. But it doesn't last long. Pasta, bread, fruit, and candy have a lot of sugar.

TASTE

You have taste buds inside your mouth. They tell you how food tastes. Most of your taste buds are on your tongue.

FAST FACT

THE HUMAN MOUTH HAS ABOUT 10,000 TASTE BUDS.

Your taste buds change often. Each one works for about 10 days. Then a new taste bud takes its place.

Super Saliva

Your taste buds need **saliva**. Food **dissolves** in your saliva. Then your taste buds can sense the flavors.

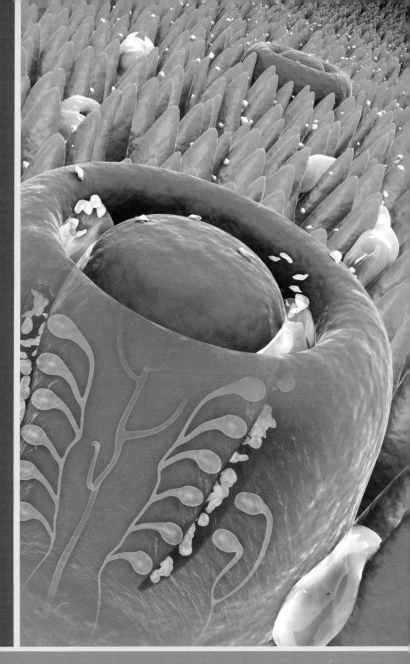

A TASTE BUD

SUGAR OR SPICE

A TASTE GUESSING GAME

WHAT YOU NEED: CUP, PLATE, SUGAR, CINNAMON, SALT, PAPER TOWELS, COTTON SWABS

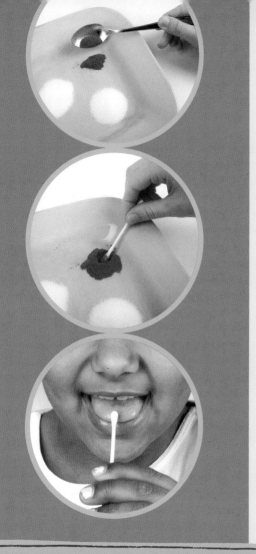

HOW TO DO IT

1. Fill the cup with water. Put a little sugar, cinnamon, and salt on the plate.

2. Wipe your tongue with a paper **towel**. Get it as dry as you can. Keep your mouth open. Pinch your nose and close your eyes.

3. Have your friend dip a cotton swab in one of the ingredients. Rub it all over your tongue. Can you tell what it is? Rinse out your mouth with water.

4. Repeat steps 2 and 3 with the other ingredients.

5. Now repeat the experiment. This time don't pinch your nose. Did something change?

WHAT'S HAPPENING?

It was hard to tell the tastes apart, right? That's because your mouth didn't have any **saliva**. The second time you could smell the ingredients. But you still couldn't taste them.

SCENTS OF
SMELL

Special cells in your nose sense odors. Nerves send messages about the odors to your brain. Then your brain tells you what the smell is.

You also smell another way. When you chew food, it creates odors. The odors go up your pharynx into your nasal cavity.

SIGNAL TO THE BRAIN

SPECIAL CELLS

NASAL CAVITY

ODOR

ODOR

MOUTH

PHARYNX

TOGETHER

Smell and taste work together. When you eat, you smell and taste at the same time.

Together, smell and taste create flavor. Flavor is how you decide what you like to eat. You won't want to eat food that has a bad flavor.

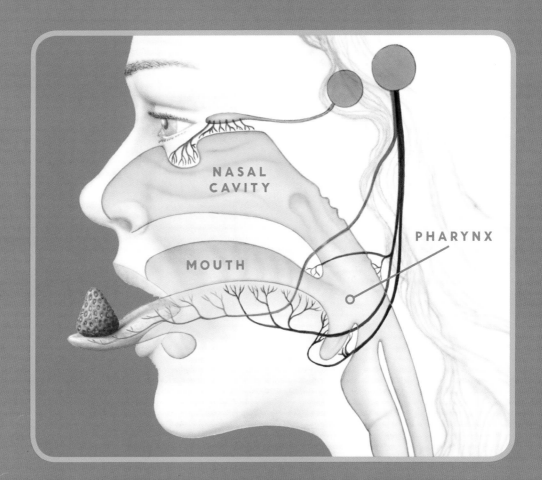

NASAL CAVITY

MOUTH

PHARYNX

THE NOSE KNOWS

SMELLING IS IMPORTANT!

WHAT YOU NEED: BANANAS, VANILLA EXTRACT, PINE NEEDLES, PENCIL SHAVINGS, CUPS, MARKER, BLINDFOLD, A FRIEND

HOW TO DO IT

1. Put each ingredient in a cup. Label each cup with the first letter of its ingredient.

2. Put a blindfold on your friend. Have your friend smell a cup. Could your friend guess what was in it? Ask your friend if he or she has any memories of the smell.

3. Repeat with the other three cups. How fast did your friend guess what was in them? Then have your friend put the blindfold on you! Can you guess what all the scents were?

WHAT'S HAPPENING?

Knowing different smells is important. Have you ever smelled something bad? Often something that is **dangerous** will smell bad. Your nose warns you not to eat it.

CHEW ON THIS

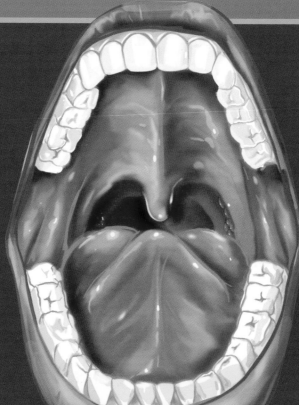

Your teeth are great for cutting and grinding food into little bits.

Your **saliva** helps too. It breaks sugars down, right inside your mouth!

Saliva also softens your food. That makes it easier to chew and swallow.

FOOD TUBE

When you are finished chewing, you swallow. Your tongue pushes the food into your pharynx. The food goes through the pharynx into a tube. It's called the esophagus. It connects to your stomach.

WRONG TUBE?

Sometimes food goes down the wrong tube!

You have one tube for breathing and another for eating. Sometimes food goes down the breathing tube. That causes choking. Choking is **dangerous**. If you see someone choking, get an adult.

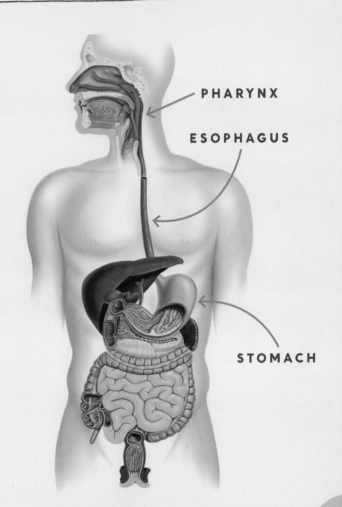

PHARYNX

ESOPHAGUS

STOMACH

STOMACH

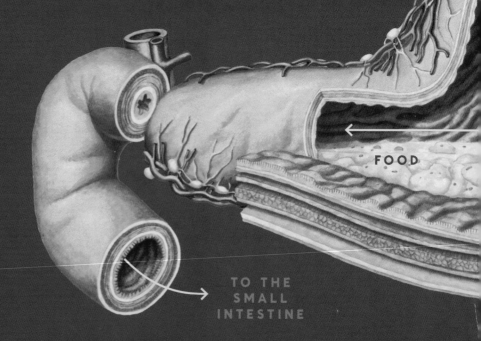

The chewed-up food falls into your stomach. Your stomach is a sack. It's made mostly of muscle. Your stomach has chemicals that mix with the food. The chemicals break down fats and proteins in the food.

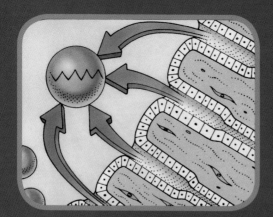

CHEMICALS LATCH ONTO PROTEINS AND BREAK THEM APART.

FOOD

TO THE
SMALL
INTESTINE

20

ESOPHAGUS

STOMACH

Then your stomach **squeezes** the food to break it into even smaller pieces. It churns like a washing machine! When the food leaves your stomach, it's mostly liquid.

BURPING

Burps can be both funny and annoying. You can't stop them!

Fizzy drinks have air in them. When you drink one, the air ends up in your stomach. Your stomach pushes it back up your throat and out your mouth. BURRRRRRP!

SMALL

INTESTINE

The stomach **squeezes** the liquid food into your small intestine. Your small intestine is a long, thin tube.

Most food digestion happens in your small intestine.

The three parts of the small intestine are the duodenum, the jejunum, and the ileum.

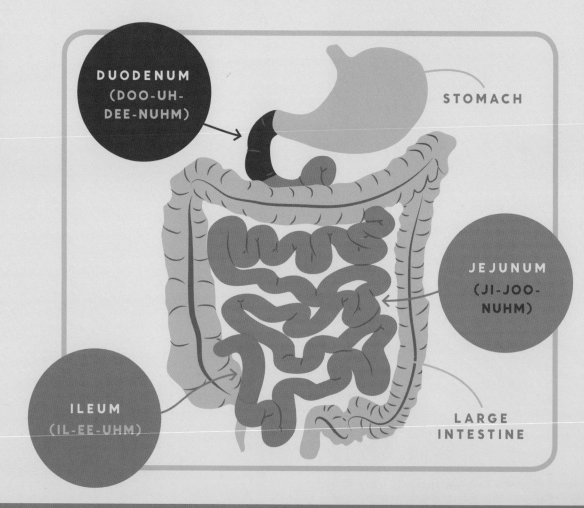

DUODENUM
(DOO-UH-
DEE-NUHM)

STOMACH

JEJUNUM
(JI-JOO-
NUHM)

ILEUM
(IL-EE-UHM)

LARGE
INTESTINE

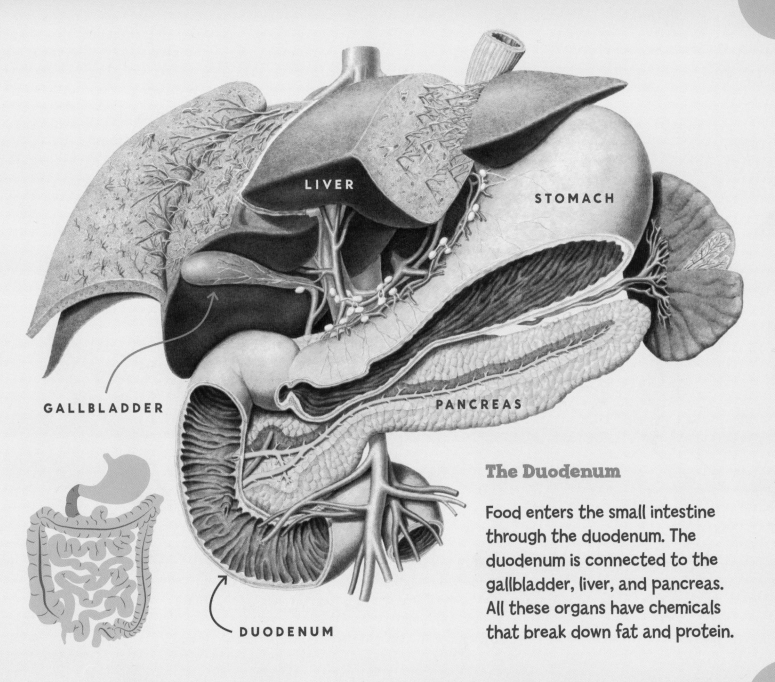

LIVER

STOMACH

GALLBLADDER

PANCREAS

DUODENUM

The Duodenum

Food enters the small intestine through the duodenum. The duodenum is connected to the gallbladder, liver, and pancreas. All these organs have chemicals that break down fat and protein.

The Jejunum

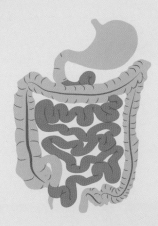

Then the food enters the jejunum. It's the longest part of your small intestine. It **absorbs nutrients** that have already been broken down.

Proteins, sugars, and fats are now small enough to fit inside your cells! They pass through the wall of the jejunum into your blood. Your blood moves them all over your body. Your cells use them for energy.

NUTRIENTS (IN RED) PASS THROUGH THE WALL OF THE INTESTINE INTO THE BLOOD.

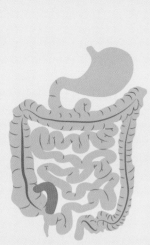

The Ileum

Then the food enters the ileum. It **absorbs** any remaining **nutrients**. It joins the small intestine to the large intestine.

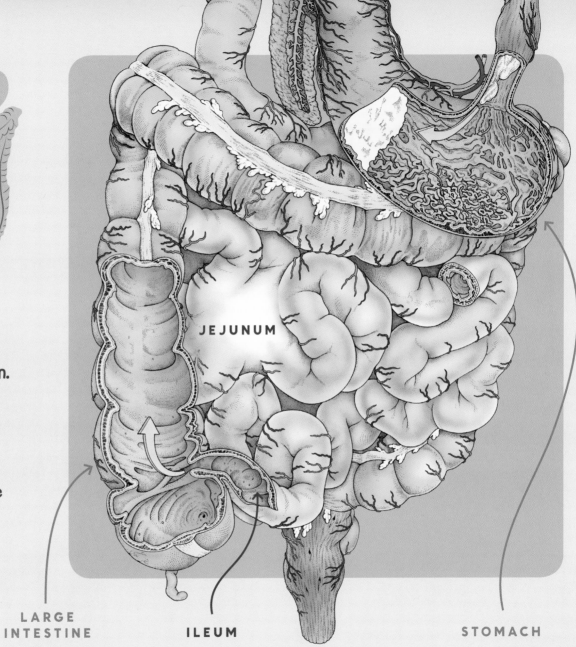

JEJUNUM

LARGE
INTESTINE

ILEUM

STOMACH

LARGE
INTESTINE

Some parts of food aren't useful to your body. These parts are waste. Your body needs to get rid of it.

The waste goes from your small intestine into your large intestine. The main part of the large intestine is the colon (KOH-LUHN). Your colon **absorbs** water from the waste. Then it moves the waste into the rectum (REK-TUHM).

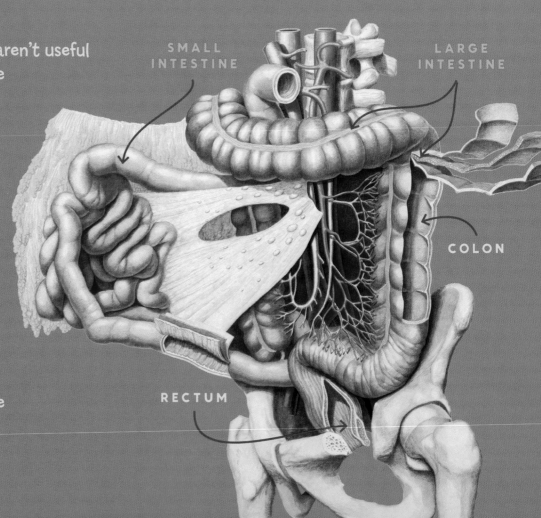

SMALL INTESTINE

LARGE INTESTINE

COLON

RECTUM

The colon has four parts.

They are the ascending colon, the transverse colon, the descending colon, and the sigmoid colon. They surround the small intestine.

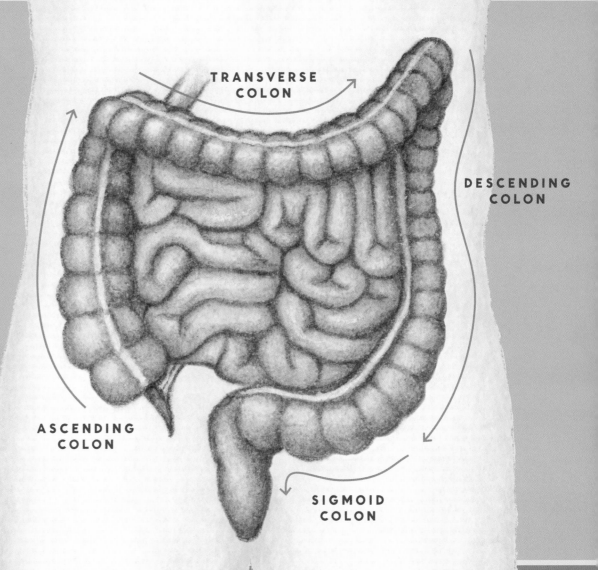

TRANSVERSE COLON

DESCENDING COLON

ASCENDING COLON

SIGMOID COLON

THE LAST STOP

F ood waste ends up in your rectum. It stays there until you're ready to poop. Then it goes through a muscle called the anus (AY-NUHSS).

The toilet is the last stop for food waste!

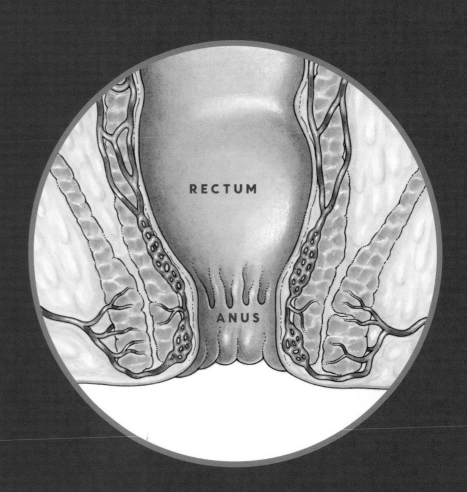

RECTUM

ANUS

Why Does Poop Stink?

Poop stinks because it has sulfur in it. Sulfur is a smelly chemical. Skunks and rotten eggs also get their smells from sulfur.

Bacteria in your colon make sulfur. It makes farts smell too!

WHAT ABOUT NUMBER ONE?

Peeing gets rid of waste from your blood.

When cells make energy from **nutrients**, they also create waste. The waste moves through your blood until it gets to your **kidneys**.

Your kidneys remove the waste from your blood. It goes into your **bladder**. Then you pee it out!

FOLLOW YOUR FOOD

SEE HOW YOU DIGEST!

WHAT YOU NEED: WHITE AND PINK TIGHTS, SCISSORS, RULER, SAFETY PINS, LARGE BOWL, PLASTIC BAG, WATER, BANANA, CRACKERS, VINEGAR, SPOON, PLASTIC GLOVES

HOW TO DO IT

1. Cut a leg off the white tights. Cut off the tip of the toe. Then cut a leg off the pink tights. Cut off a 6-inch (15 cm) section.

2. Put the pink section over the white leg. Line up one edge of the pink section with the top of the white leg. Turn the edges back. Fold them twice. Put pins around the edge to hold it. Pull the other end of the pink tights over the safety pins.

3. Put some water, banana, and crackers in the plastic bag. **Squeeze** the bag to mash the food and water together. Add three spoonfuls of vinegar.

4. Cut a hole in the plastic bag. Put the open toe of the white tights over the hole. Put the end of the pink tights in the bowl. Have a friend squeeze the bag. The food goes down to the bowl. Some should seep through the sides of the tights.

WHAT'S HAPPENING?

You made a model of digestion! The bag is the stomach. The vinegar is the stomach chemicals. The white leg is the small intestine. The pink leg is the large intestine. The stuff that seeps through the tights is the **nutrients**. The food in the bowl is poop.

ABSORB - to soak up or take in.

BEAN - a seed or a pod that you can eat.

BLADDER - the organ in the body that stores urine.

DANGEROUS - able or likely to cause harm or injury.

DISSOLVE - to mix with a liquid so that it becomes part of the liquid.

KIDNEY - the organ in the body that turns waste from the blood into urine.

NUTRIENT - something that helps living things grow. Vitamins, minerals, and proteins are nutrients.

SALIVA - the watery liquid produced by glands in your mouth.

SQUEEZE - to press or grip something tightly.

TOWEL - a cloth or paper used for cleaning or drying.

GLOSSARY